LOVE AND OTHER POEMS

LOVE AND OTHER POEMS
ALEX DIMITROV

COPPER CANYON PRESS
PORT TOWNSEND, WASHINGTON

Cover art: Felix Gonzalez-Torres, "Untitled", 1989. C-print jigsaw puzzle in plastic bag, 7½ x 9½ in. Edition of 2, 1 AP. Image courtesy of Andrea Rosen Gallery. Photographer: Lance Brewer. © Felix Gonzalez-Torres. Courtesy of The Felix Gonzalez-Torres Foundation.

Copper Canyon Press is in residence at Fort Worden State Park in Port Townsend, Washington, under the auspices of Centrum. Centrum is a gathering place for artists and creative thinkers from around the world, students of all ages and backgrounds, and audiences seeking extraordinary cultural enrichment.

LIBRARY OF CONGRESS CATALOGING-IN-PUBLICATION DATA
Names: Dimitrov, Alex, author.
Title: Love and other poems / Alex Dimitrov.
Description: Port Townsend, Washington : Copper Canyon Press, [2021] |
    Summary: "A collection of poems by Alex Dimitrov"—Provided by
    publisher.
Identifiers: LCCN 2020030228 | ISBN 9781556595998 (paperback)
Subjects: LCGFT: Poetry.
Classification: LCC PS3604.I4648 L68 2021 | DDC 811/.6—dc23
LC record available at https://lccn.loc.gov/2020030228

98765432 FIRST PRINTING

COPPER CANYON PRESS
Post Office Box 271
Port Townsend, Washington 98368
www.coppercanyonpress.org

This book is for our city of New York

All I want is boundless love.

Frank O'Hara

CONTENTS

I don't want to sound unreasonable
but I need to be in love immediately.
I can't watch this sunset
on 14th Street by myself.
Everyone is walking fast
right after therapy, texting back
their lovers orange hearts
and unicorns—it's insane to me.
They're missing this free sunset
willingly! Or even worse
they're going home to cook
and read this sad poem online.
Let me tell you something,
people have quit smoking.
They don't get drinks
but they juice. There are
way too many photos
and most all of us look better
in them than we do in life.
What happened? This is
truly so embarrassing!
I want to make a case
for 1440 minutes every day
where we stop whatever else
is going on and look each other
in the eyes. Like dogs.
Like morning newspapers
in evening light. So long!
So much for this short drama.
We will die one day
and our cheap headlines
won't apply to anything.

The internet will be forgotten.
All the praise and pandering.
I'd really rather take a hike
and by the way, I'm gay.
The sunset too is homosexual.
At least today, between
the buildings which are moody
and the trees (which honestly)
they look a bit unhealthy here.
They're anxious. They're concerned.
They're wondering why
I'm broke and lonely
in Manhattan—though of course
I'll never say it—and besides
it's almost spring. It's fine.
It's goth. Hello! The truth is
no one will remember us.
We're only specks of dust
or one—one speck of dust.
Some brutes who screamed
for everything to look at us.
Well, look at us. Still terrible
and awful. Awful and pretending
we're not terrible. Such righteous
saints! Repeating easy lines,
performing our great politics.
It's just so very boring,
the real mystery in fact
is how we managed to make room
for love at all. Punk rock,
avant-garde cinema.
I love you, reader
but you should know
the sunset's over now.

I'm standing right in front of
Nowhere bar, dehydrated
and quite scared
but absolutely willing
to keep going. It makes sense
you do the same. It's far
too late for crying and quite
useless too. You can be sad
and still look so good. You can
say New York is beautiful
and it wouldn't be a headline
and it wouldn't be a lie.
Just take a cab and not the 6,
it's never once in ten years
been on time. It's orbiting
some other world
where there are sunsets
every hour and no money
and no us—that's luck!
The way to get there
clearly wasn't written down.
Don't let that stop you though.
Look at the sky. Kiss everyone
you can for sure.

I

Part of the celestial sky known as the sea.
Where there's little of Earth
and nothing of us as these forms.
In the animal soup of time beside the Water Bearer
and the Great River. They're up there for the lost
with Polaris. In the oceans. At home.
In your own body which is mostly water
and mostly not yours. Not even tonight
while you're in it. When another body
sleeps alongside all your want.
What does the moon know of our language,
our care for its perceived loneliness
which may be its one joy.
Where would you find love if not on the earth?
As if we should be permitted elsewhere.
As if we understand our own wars,
our reasons for fleeing, forgetting—
the history we do not allow ourselves to imagine
and the lives we refuse to know,
which are often our own. I think of you here,
where you haven't been in years.
There's a flaw in the wood of the door
or my own madness that welcomes the wind
although it is summer, although I am winter.
You could see the sea from the desert
on a night when no one comes to harm you,
an evening when bombs go off somewhere as planned.
We could be letters. Sent here
to warn each other of a much better time.
We could be no one. And for nothing.
For what?

The living looking for eternity
don't know eternity is brief.
A favorite thing about being alive
or other questions no one asks me,
and it would be knowing people.
Knowledge through time.
What's the name of that hour in the day
where no matter our planned futures
everything is full of nothing
as the world is full of people
without reason other than small chance.
You are tired and most singular
in the middle of the afternoon
when seeing you on the street
(and not in a bedroom) reminds me you're real,
allowing me to begin the rest of this poem.
Because life isn't enough
which is unbelievable to the fog, sea,
or anything lucky to be
without our incurable consciousness.
Vanishing. A once-orange leaf that's been
left in a book. The silver handles
of the casket as it's lowered into the earth.
People's mistakes. Dark matter.
The sky just before evening.
One boat in the Atlantic.
A handful of balloons going all the way up.
The few places in the world where it's raining
as you read this. As I write this.
As I read this out loud and somewhere
what is expected does not return.
The last lamp in an old house.

How I'm not sure if I'd like to end on an image
of someone turning it on, turning it off.
Silences. Between the waves and beneath them.
People's mistakes. People's mistakes.

1969

The summer everyone left for the moon
even those yet to be born. And the dead
who can't vacation here but met us all there
by the veil between worlds. The No. 1 song
in America was "In the Year 2525"
because who has ever lived in the present
when there's so much of the future
to continue without us.
How the best lover won't need to forgive you
and surely take everything off your hands
without having to ask, without knowing
your name, no matter the number of times
you married or didn't, your favorite midnight movie,
the cigarettes you couldn't give up,
wanting to kiss other people you shouldn't
and now to forever be kissed by the earth.
In the earth. With the earth.
When we all briefly left it
to look back on each other from above,
shocked by how bright even our pain is
running wildly beside us like an underground river.
And whatever language is good for,
a sign, a message left up there that reads:
"Here men from planet Earth first set foot
upon the moon, July 1969 A.D.
We came in peace for all mankind."
Then returned to continue the war.

WAITING AT STONEWALL

It's a Friday in New York
and fifty years from '69.
Though since we've yet to meet
or have, and are still looking,
what we've said to each other
in photos and films, bars
and basements, returns
with enough echo
to remind us of ourselves.
Those of us who resisted heroes
and sentiment. Those of us
who waited and found neither—
not the promised liberation
in marriage, or the salvation
of laws. How some asked
to carry America's guns
and did. How others knew
equality was a rumor,
elusive as freedom or sex.
Do you think about dying
every time you have sex?
I still think about dying.
I do think about death.
Or a day in childhood when I saw
the only place I could live
was here. Inside.
So whoever wanted me
had to come through the body.
Which has rarely been beautiful
to me. Too soft and unconvincing.
Too small. I hope the future
is free of god and memory.

I hope the future is
all body, all blood.
And since to be queer
is a way to forgive life,
I'll take as long as I want
finishing my cigarette on Seventh,
walking up Christopher
and thinking of everyone
who's yet to get here—
somewhere in a bedroom maybe,
young and bored across
the country, not impressed
by our parades or idols,
all the sponsorship we bought.
I'm late for a drink but wander,
handsome and aimless,
looking for a sign
before nodding to the dead
who always need a light.

TIME

Again I am unprepared
standing under an awning
in the middle of summer

autumn, winter, spring—
watching the downpour
in what could be

the middle of life;
wondering how long I'll wait
before becoming the rain.

LOVE

I love you early in the morning and it's difficult to love you.

I love the January sky and knowing it will change although unlike us.

I love watching people read.

I love photo booths.

I love midnight.

I love writing letters and this is my letter. To the world that never wrote to me.

I love snow and briefly.

I love the first minutes in a warm room after stepping out of the cold.

I love my twenties and want them back every day.

I love time.

I love people.

I love people and my time away from them the most.

I love the part of my desk that's darkened by my elbows.

I love feeling nothing but relief during the chorus of a song.

I love space.

I love every planet.

I love the big unknowns but need to know who called or wrote, who's coming—if they want the same things I do, if they want much less.

I love not loving Valentine's Day.

I love how February is the shortest month.

I love that Barack Obama was president.

I love the quick, charged time between two people smoking a cigarette outside a bar.

I love everyone on Friday night.

I love New York City.

I love New York City a lot.

I love that day in childhood when I thought I was someone else.

I love wondering how animals perceive our daily failures.

I love the lines in *Cat on a Hot Tin Roof* when Brick's father says, "Life is important. There's nothing else to hold onto."

I love Brick.

I love that we can fail at love and continue to live.

I love writing this and not knowing what I'll love next.

I love looking at paintings and being reminded I am alive.

I love Turner's paintings and the sublime.

I love the coming of spring even in the most withholding March.

I love skipping anything casual—"hi, how are you, it's been forever"—and getting straight to the center of pain. Or happiness.

I love opening a window in a room.

I love the feeling of possibility by the end of the first cup of coffee.

I love hearing anyone listen to Nina Simone.

I love Nina Simone.

I love how we can choose our own families.

I love when no one knows where I am but feel terrified to be forgotten.

I love Saturdays.

I love that despite our mistakes this will end.

I love how people get on planes to New York and California.

I love the hour after rain and the beginning of the cruelest month.

I love imagining Weldon Kees on a secret island.

I love the beach on a cloudy day.

I love never being disappointed by chocolate.

I love that morning when I was twenty and had just met someone very important (though I didn't know it) and I walked down an almost empty State Street because it was still early and not at all late—and of course I could change everything (though I also didn't know it)—I could find anyone, go anywhere, I wasn't sorry for who I was.

I love the impulse to change.

I love seeing what we do with what we can't change.

I love the moon's independent indifference.

I love walking the same streets as Warhol.

I love what losing something does but I don't love losing it.

I love how the past shifts when there's more.

I love kissing.

I love hailing a cab and going home alone.

I love being surprised by May although it happens every year.

I love closing down anything—a bar, restaurant, party—and that time between late night and dawn when one lamp goes on wherever you are and you know. You know what you know even if it's hard to know it.

I love being a poet.

I love all poets.

I love Jim Morrison for saying, "I'd like to do a song or a piece of music that's just a pure expression of joy, like a celebration of existence, like the coming of spring or the sun rising, just pure unbounded joy. I don't think we've really done that yet."

I love everything I haven't done.

I love looking at someone without need or panic.

I love the quiet of the trees in a new city.

I love how the sky is connected to a part of us that understands something big and knows nothing about it too.

I love the minutes before you're about to see someone you love.

I love any film that delays resolution.

I love being in a cemetery because judgment can't live there.

I love being on a highway in June or anytime at all.

I love magic.

I love the zodiac.

I love all of my past lives.

I love that hour of the party when everyone's settled into their discomfort and someone tells you something really important—in passing—because it's too painful any other way.

I love the last moments before sleep.

I love the promise of summer.

I love going to the theater and seeing who we are.

I love glamour—shamelessly—and all glamour. Which is not needed to live but shows people love life. What else is it there for? Why not ask for more?

I love red shoes.

I love black leather.

I love the grotesque ways in which people eat ice cream—on sidewalks, alone—however they need it, whenever they feel free enough.

I love being in the middle of a novel.

I love how mostly everyone in Jane Austen is looking for love.

I love July and its slowness.

I love the idea of liberation and think about it all the time.

I love imagining a world without money.

I love imagining a life with enough money to write when I want.

I love standing in front of the ocean.

I love that sooner or later we forget even "the important things."

I love how people write in the sand, on buildings, on paper. Their own bodies. Fogged mirrors. Texts they'll draft but never send.

I love silence.

I love owning a velvet cape and not knowing how to cook.

I love that instant when an arc of light passes through a room and I'm reminded that everything really is moving.

I love August and its sadness.

I love Sunday for that, too.

I love jumping in a pool and how somewhere on the way up your body relaxes and accepts the shock of the water.

I love Paris for being Paris.

I love Godard's films.

I love any place that makes room for loneliness.

I love how the Universe is 95% dark matter and energy and somewhere in the rest of it there is us.

I love bookstores and the autonomy when I'm in one.

I love that despite my distrust in politics I am able to vote.

I love wherever my friends are.

I love voting though know art and not power is what changes human character.

I love what seems to me the discerning nature of cats.

I love the often-uncomplicated joy of dogs.

I love Robert Lax for living alone.

I love the extra glass of wine happening somewhere, right now.

I love schools and teachers.

I love September and how we see it as a way to begin.

I love knowledge. Even the fatal kind. Even the one without "use value."

I love getting dressed more than getting undressed.

I love mystery.

I love lighting candles.

I love religious spaces though I'm sometimes lost there.

I love the sun for worshipping no one.

I love the sun for showing up every day.

I love the felt order after a morning of errands.

I love walking toward nowhere in particular and the short-lived chance of finding something new.

I love people who smile only when moved to.

I love that a day on Venus lasts longer than a year.

I love Whitman for writing, "the fever of doubtful news, the fitful events; / These come to me days and nights and go from me again, / But they are not the Me myself."

I love October when the veil between worlds is thinnest.

I love how at any moment I could forgive someone from the past.

I love the wind and how we never see it.

I love the performed sincerity in pornography and wonder if its embarrassing transparency is worth adopting in other parts of life.

I love how magnified emotions are at airports.

I love dreams. Conscious and unconscious. Lived and not yet.

I love anyone who risks their life for their ideal one.

I love Marsha P. Johnson and Sylvia Rivera.

I love how people make art even in times of impossible pain.

I love all animals.

I love ghosts.

I love that we continue to invent meaning.

I love the blue hours between three and five when Plath wrote *Ariel*.

I love that despite having one body there are many ways to live.

I love November because I was born there.

I love people who teach children that most holidays are a product of capitalism and have little to do with love—which would never celebrate massacre—which would never care about money or greed.

I love people who've quit their jobs to be artists.

I love you for reading this as opposed to anything else.

I love the nostalgia of the future.

I love that the tallest mountain in our solar system is safe and on Mars.

I love dancing.

I love being in love with the wrong people.

I love that in the fall of 1922 Virginia Woolf wrote, "We have bitten off a large piece of life—but why not? Did I not make out a philosophy some time ago which comes to this—that one must always be on the move?"

I love how athletes believe in the body and know it will fail them.

I love dessert for breakfast.

I love all of the dead.

I love gardens.

I love holding my breath underwater.

I love whoever it is untying our shoes.

I love that December is summer in Australia.

I love statues in a downpour.

I love how no matter where on the island, at any hour, there's at least one lit square at the top or bottom of a building in Manhattan.

I love diners.

I love that the stars can't be touched.

I love getting in a car and turning the keys just to hear music.

I love ritual.

I love chance, too.

I love people who have quietly survived being misunderstood yet remain kids.

And yes, I love that Marilyn Monroe requested Judy Garland's "Over the Rainbow" to be played at her funeral. And her casket was lined in champagne satin. And Lee Strasberg ended the eulogy by saying, "I cannot say goodbye. Marilyn never liked goodbyes, but in the peculiar way she had of turning things around so that they faced reality, I will say au revoir."

I love the different ways we have of saying the same thing.

I love anyone who cannot say goodbye.

ONCE

Would you even believe
when it finally happens

how easy it is to feel
without any proof

that love may be, could be, actually is
longer than time.

JUNE

There will never be more of summer
than there is now. Walking alone
through Union Square I am carrying flowers
and the first rosé to a party where I'm expected.
It's Sunday and the trains run on time
but today death feels so far, it's impossible
to go underground. I would like to say
something to everyone I see (an entire
city) but I'm unsure what it is yet.
Each time I leave my apartment
there's at least one person crying,
reading, or shouting after a stranger
anywhere along my commute.
It's possible to be happy alone,
I say out loud and to no one
so it's obvious, and now here
in the middle of this poem.
Rarely have I felt more charmed
than on Ninth Street, watching a woman
stop in the middle of the sidewalk
to pull up her hair like it's
an emergency—and it is.
People do know they're alive.
They hardly know what to do with themselves.
I almost want to invite her with me
but I've passed and yes it'd be crazy
like trying to be a poet, trying to be anyone here.
How do you continue to love New York,
my friend who left for California asks me.
It's awful in the summer and winter,
and spring and fall last maybe two weeks.
This is true. It's all true, of course,

like my preference for difficult men
which I had until recently
because at last, for one summer
the only difficulty I'm willing to imagine
is walking through this first humid day
with my hands full, not at all peaceful
but entirely possible and real.

RIVER PHOENIX

In my own private Idaho
I'm in bed with River Phoenix
chain-smoking and talking about the afterlife.
He's about to give up being famous,
I'm about to make him one more drink.
When I die, he says, looking at the way
I look at him, *it'll be a glorious day.*
It'll probably be a waterfall.
And because there's so much water
in living, I help take his shirt off
right here on the earth.
Me and him. You and you.
Reading this to see if I'm acting,
if I'm really myself, if I'm good at pretending.
Why would we be here then, in bed together,
asking each other what the way back is
in case we happen to change our minds.

SUMMER SOLSTICE

Again it's the longest day of the year.
What finds you assumes its place
in the morning and stays.
Like the sidewalk flowers
refusing death in the heat.
Even they see one childhood
is already behind you.
You've lived long enough
to be less stunned (and foolishly)
by how afternoon slows like a swimmer
holding anything the sun becomes.
People go in and out of the day—
returning—sometimes with less
of what no one promised them.
Nights continue. Love is hard to account for.
This is what summer has always been
and where limerence goes on.
And this is the light that arrives
despite everything. It is the most light.
It will happen more often than you expect.

JULY

At last it's impossible to think of anything
as I swim through the heat on Broadway
and disappear in the Strand. Nobody
on these shelves knows who I am
but I feel so seen, it's easy to be aimless
not having written a line for weeks.
Outside New York continues to be New York.
I was half expecting it to be LA
but no luck. No luck with the guy
I'm seeing, no luck with money,
no luck with becoming a saint.
I do not want you, perfect life.
I decided to stay a poet long ago,
I know what I'm in for. And still
the free space of the sky
lures me back out—not even
canonical beauty can keep me inside
(and beauty, I'm done with you too).
I guess after all I'll take love—
sweeping, all-consuming,
grandiose love. Don't just call
or ask to go to a movie.
That's off my list too!
I want absolutely everything
on this Friday afternoon
when not one person is looking for me.
I'm crazy and lonely.
I've never been boring.
And believe it or not, I'm all I want.

THE SUN

At once stunning and perilous
to be under it. To understand
your body's place in the order of living
by the number of trips it makes around a star.
To see it every day without choice,
more than any friend or lover.
More than your own face
on weeks you're lucky
to consult a mirror less.
And some nights, the luck
more than the will to live.
Knowing exactly when it will return,
unlike most obsessions.
How it feels to be addressed by it:
never asking you to speak of
the real shame and wonder
lining the skin almost always,
the ridiculous desire to feel.
Many before have worshipped it.
Followed it anywhere
in that exacting brightness, slow
then finally impossible to endure.
Like a love affair that kept you alive
for so long and recovered
the person you were before evening,
before fog. The life you only recognize
by having had light at all.

NEW MOON

Wherever you are tonight
and whoever is with you,
small fist the earth is
if one new moon can charm us.
It likely won't change you this once
or resolve your real worry
about romance and death, friendship
and time, the narrow hallways
we'll walk unaccompanied
by anyone we know.
It is not too late for ardor.
It is not yet late enough for less.
What could fill description
like the moon or New York City?
Maybe chance and every river,
how our mothers look in spring.
It's motherless up there. Then quiet.
And our names—the names
we tried so hard to live with—
are no longer ours. They're
just sound. They're mere color.
They have never wanted us less.

AUGUST

So this is love. When it slows
the rain touches everyone on their way home.
Whatever was promised of pleasure
costs the body more than it has.
Perhaps they were right in putting love into books…
to look at the sky without asking a question,
to look at the sea and know you won't drown today.
Despite all our work, even the worst of life
has a place in memory. And the fixed hours
between two and five before evening
are the aimless future with someone
who cannot stay new. August returns us
to a gap in history where our errors
find the invention of a kinder regret.
Almost possible: to believe these days
will change more than us but the past, too.
Which is blue and without end.
A long drive toward a remembered place.
A secret left on a beach. Underwater
where the voices of summer are tones of speech,
requiring less of the mind. The familiar creaks
in the old floorboards. Glasses left out in the storm.
Our handwritten lists with every illegible worry
and yes. The person you think of
despite their cruelty. The sun and its cruelty.
How it's kept its distance and kept us alive.
Not needing to know anything about what we do
with the rest of desire.

MY SECRET

I'm suddenly
one of those people
who goes out
to dinner alone.
The wind around
the Chelsea Piers
is warm tonight.
A dog on 10th Avenue
barks so loud
I can feel it,
clawing at
some part of me
refusing people
but okay with trees.
There are still so many
things I wouldn't mind
forgetting. Like the mail
key I keep losing
or the plant
I almost bought
but knew I'd kill.
Everyone I love
is disappointed in me.
I don't text or call
or ever make real plans.
I'm so sorry everybody!
I am truly trying
to run into you
so casually
and overdressed,
there'd be no shame
in our admitting

we are animals
and need each other.
No shame in how we're
only terrible at life.
Especially because
(speaking for me)
I am sadder than
I look but happier
than all the dead.
And if you've seen
how small we are
in NASA's photos,
it's impossible to
think our happiness
is that important.
To order red
and not want
all of you to come
because it is.

IMPERMANENCE

The first ending. And knowing it would end
I wanted another. Lover, summer,
pen with which to write it all down.
The first disappointment. Which is not
remembered but lives in the body.
And how familiar it became. To take
the same walk home or lean over ledges,
to say my own name when meeting someone.
Again and again for the last time:
the taste of salt in the afternoon.
Flowers for no one—alive and sold on the street.
What did I think was promised in being?
The way a stranger can finish you off.
Once only. And never the same
after that. After knowledge.
How people are being detained
and shot with our money.
All of which cannot prepare us for death
of which I am a student
and which is this country's business:
the permanence of others.
Even our cruelty toward one another.
Will end. And I know
that looking at the night sky
is me looking at the past. At light
that's long escaped and travels alone
but won't always.

GOLDEN RECORD

I

What will you miss of Earth
if we're headed somewhere

      without maps or seasons
      between nowhere and eternity.

First door—second—and a third that did not free you.

August in which someone you will know for years is born.

Like the ultimate quiet moment of my life
said Gene Cernan
        of being the last man on the moon.

      Your childhood house and how it's somehow ageless.
      The light on the ocean in the middle of the day

when no one appears to be looking
and people have memorized their lives so well

          they forget them.

They forget that we're here.

II

And the past   that happens there
seems unbelievable   everything
though we know   though we know
everything   seems unbelievable
that happens there   And the past

III

A pigeon loudly flying through the cathedral

where a funeral arrives
       and they've prepared the body

(how death too can be interrupted

             though not changed).

And with luck

       we're somehow out there on a golden record
       since the same year Carter entered office

the year that Callas, Crawford died

             and Milk was San Francisco's.

       Our one history of Earth
stamped various and frozen on a 12-inch copper disc

      all gold—a greatest hits from the beginning until then—

      as if we could be summary

             and are

and may be nothing too but nothing.

IV

Through space   in that they won't be back
the *Voyagers*   are remarkable
like people   like people
are remarkable   the *Voyagers*
in that they won't be back   Through space

V

Scenes from our world:

                 the Taj Mahal

a school of fish   sunset with birds

        old man with dog and flowers.

The sound of a kiss

        on the short list of sounds

not quite telling

                who we are

                                and were

        (if there is more than us

                it isn't silence that describes Earth).

"Melancholy Blues" and *Rite of Spring*,
        a night chant or a wedding song
                a raga

and the Brandenburg Concerto finally playing to the stars

beyond them   and whatever's after

    like a child might ask—

        a small romance we cannot paint

          despite

      and if

              perhaps

even the chance of telling someone who we were compels us.

In the words of *Voyager*'s gold record

          if it ever plays:

Good night ladies and gentlemen. Goodbye and see you next time.

REHEARSALS

I continue to be that person
who thinks enough of the future
to let it into the foyer without opening the door.

One summer
eating a peach and wearing a shirt of mine
you sky almost lower bright harp.

Should we leave ourselves
inside the longer nights we'd see it,
even as the days feel once again
like welcome obligation.
And the leaves die
entering a stranger beauty,
knowing nothing of our troubles
or the lust to grieve.
Stepping onto a train. Returning.
The first kiss outside the door
where the keys hang unturned.
Arriving. To the windows at noon
and the sheets from whatever
was felt of the body.
Then forgotten. Then the flowers
carried up five flights of stairs
and like knowledge
changing a room
almost slightly.
With the photograph
to remember the light
which appears gold and isn't.
Is even less so when caught.
Regardless, we do it again and again
as the old ghosts lift and someone
unafraid of who we are calls back.
In the new moon, with the low wind
how no one exists alone.
The dead too have each other to look for.
Like the scent of late fire clinging to hair
and the keys now finding their locks
before we go in.

Somehow everything I've almost known
and everything I won't is in the photo.
Taken 3.7 billion miles from Earth,
of Earth, and all that isn't Earth or ours.
Every book read for pleasure, as compass.
Thousands of cups of coffee,
first dates, missed phone calls—
happening right there in blue
and easy to overlook
if like me you're distracted
by the bands of sunlight
disrupting deep space.
Ridiculous how maybe
there's nowhere else
for even our fantasies to play out.
They must start and stay here,
regardless of how obvious
we become to ourselves
in daily apathy or pleasure.
I may wake up tomorrow
and write poems
because I'm terrified of dying.
You might take up
the business of death
and build coffins, who knows.
What would you say was the earth then?
If someone asked you to describe it
once and without revision.
Like a question from a childhood game
or those moments in a photo booth
when you see yourself lit up,
nothing like what you imagined.

Though there's something true
about those photos.
Something true about doing it
once and without revision.

ZENITH

Now I will always be older than Jesus.
And the secrets I'm saving will also continue
like nights we were so much ourselves
they're forgotten, they occur twice.
Not unlike the day I keep trying to find
when I invite death for a walk
on which there's no obvious season,
and even the sky won't house
the short distance between us
as we follow each other and talk
of everything we have in common.
The cold morning without morning.

OCTOBER

A different smell of dirt.
The walk between
every appointment now quicker.
And clouds—in all their indifference—
somehow looking at you.
Aren't you, too, unbelievable.
Aren't you simply a you.
No doubt, as Woolf wrote
one October on Paradise Road:
the extremely insignificant position I have
in this important world. Choosing words
that won't obscure how punishing we are.
Setting the alarm and keeping the eyes open.
Long. Into the dark. Or the wind—
suddenly matching our need
to change. The garment
with last year's stain faded but there.
Of course it is cold now
but somewhere it's colder.
People don't know what to do
with their hair, all their fear.
When you see the world,
introduce yourself like a guest.
Like a drop of paint outside canvas.
A dog barking for no one to hear.

YES

We have always been lonely.

NO

We're not allowed even loneliness long.

No later than now could we find an ending
for what would have been rivers.
And how someone forgot to wish us well,
and how surely we went on even if they had.
What do you remember of the future?
Reading the news has not prepared me for myself
though I must look busy. Chasing a lover,
some friends, my entire family
and somehow I've ended up here.
Perhaps how the planets must feel
as they look at each other,
far enough to tell any secret
as we're close enough
to say nothing about ourselves
and continue to live. And why?
Is the first snow just snow.
It feels like more. It leaves an impression.
I leave the bed without you,
I've chosen to leave more than that, too.
Enough of despair!
This is the red sweater I wear to the party,
vying for attention. Hailing a cab home
where it's never once taken me.
I was made here but it could have been anywhere.
That's the thing—the details—
the details promising meaning don't hold.
They've seldom been whole.
A beautiful couple still captivates me.
Long dinners extend life.
It's often the truth
that we have to be people, what else.
And I'm saving something

for next time I see you
so please do remind me,
I do want to tell you.
It was always November there.

FULL MOON

Wherever you are tonight
at exactly this hour,
look up at the sky
as you wander alone
wearing your life
like a coat in July.
It won't take long
to see the full moon
or how little there is to know
about the future,
the constellations and years
freeing no one, marking up
the night then dissolving
only to follow us into sleep.
It's the opposite of Hollywood,
religion, the pursuit of money.
There's no contract up there
but anonymity and movement.
The cold orbiting the new.
Inevitable and having arrived
so many times before,
it refuses our panic.
Our excessive desires—
how if anything out there
had these, our bodies,
they too may indulge them.
They too may ask
for everything, all the time
until there is less
and then nothing: again.

A TRUE ACCOUNT OF TALKING TO THE MOON
AT FIRE ISLAND

The moon woke me up last night,
loud and clear, saying "Hey!
I've been trying to wake you up
for fifteen minutes. Don't be so rude.
You're only the second poet
I've ever chosen to speak to personally."
Well, I couldn't believe it.
It didn't matter anymore that my books
have never been nominated for anything
or that I've wasted so much time
talking to men who don't understand me.
This was the moon! Talking to me.
Flirting even! The moon was proving
every single grant organization wrong,
the total of grants I've received
in my entire life being zero—
and here it was, my time to shine.
Literally! I didn't even have to
climb a mountain or have an epiphany.
I'm not athletic in the least,
I said to the moon. I can barely
run the reservoir in Central Park
and the only reason I like that
is because I can't tell if anyone's
emailed me while I'm running.
I'm a very gay runner, you see.
Always checking out dads
and listening to Britney on repeat.
I like to wear purple and black.
I like to feel sexy.
"What in the actual fuck,"

said the moon. "You need
so much help. You need
an NEA, a Guggenheim,
a National Book Award."
No! I said to the moon.
I only need you, baby.
Or a rich lawyer who
will play with my hair
and pay for dinners at the Odeon.
"Seriously, Alex?"
The moon looked at me
in a very stern way.
Kind of a bitch, if you ask me.
"Go to bed immediately.
In the morning I want you
to get up and write 300 poems.
I want you to keep writing poems
no matter what. Don't think about
anything else. Not even lawyers."
Okay, I said. Okay, moon.
Who knew you were such a top.
I was practically shaking.
And even though nothing good
had happened to me in the last year
and I was so sad about my life
and my poems, I went to bed
feeling loved and appreciated.
How many other poets
have talked to the moon?
Not even Frank O'Hara.
All he got was the sun.
And here I was,
the center of all beauty!

Writing these poems!
Imagine!

MORE

How again after months there is awe.
The most personal moment of the day
appears unannounced. People wear leather.
People refuse to die. There are strangers
who look like they could know your name.
And the smell of a bar on a cold night,
or the sound of traffic as it follows you home.
Sirens. Parties. How balconies hold us.
Whatever enough is, it hasn't arrived.
And on some dead afternoon
when you'll likely forget this,
as you browse through the vintage
again and again—there it is,
what everyone's given up
just to stay here. Jeweled hairpins,
scratched records, their fast youth.
Everything they've given up
to stay here and find more.

III

is even better than a regular Coke
because in New York the streets are so skinny
I'm always worried about my hair
walking down Lex in the morning
or if we'll ever get universal healthcare
and I can be assured I'm dying
in all the regular ways—nothing unusual!—
by a professional who touches me
lightly on the chest, the first time
I've been touched in months
so I consider falling in love after.
Oh god, Alex…
what is wrong with you?
I can't believe this is the title
of your poem. If you look up
the billboards are sexy and American,
letting you forget all the cruel things
you've said to your boyfriends.
There are other things
I need you to remember.
Like please stop taking cabs
so you won't have to take out a loan
or become a lawyer. And please stop
having sex with men who are terrified
of looking at your face when you cry.
One day your choices will be limited
and you'll wear the same outfit
forever into the beyond, into the gold sea.
I'm going to bury you in a white suit,
infinitely delicate and infinitely expensive
as Plath wrote, as you are,
as you've been even on bad days.

Here—this is the love poem no one
gave you. And thank god!
They couldn't do it like this.
Not only will we drink Diet Coke
in this poem, I'm also taking us
to Barneys so you can flirt
with the tall boy selling sneakers
and talking very slowly
about his gentle sword tattoo.
People of the world! Don't stop.
Don't give up style, irony, or Manhattans.
Don't apologize for wanting to fuck
someone new because you need
to feel alive. I get it! I've been there!
I'm imagining you reading this
with a phone in your hand, in your room,
by a desk, on a train or a platform.
Don't wait to do what you want!
This is what I've wanted to say
from the first line. Don't wait
because people do not have the answer.
I've written this ending before
in a book called *American Boys*
but I'll write it again for anyone
who wasn't paying attention
or talking shit about me on the internet.
I'll never get over the fact
that the buildings all light up at night,
and the night comes every night
and without regret we let it go.
We sleep a little and we live.
That's what we do.

FOR THE CRITICS

No, you never got me.
No, I don't think that you ever did.
When I walk into a bodega
and buy cigarettes and ice cream,
blueberries and Diet Coke,
all so I can cry with real enthusiasm
and with feeling, just as soon
as I can make it home—
that's called performance art.
That's performance art, you fucks.

NEW YORK

New York is the best city to cry in.

I've cried on the corner of Spring and Greene
smoking one cigarette after another,
taking two-hour lunch breaks in 2006
at my first internship at *Interview* magazine.

I cried in Washington Square Park the other night
thinking about healthcare
and how I quit my job to write poetry,
and how even a job in poetry
prevents you from writing it.

I've cried so many times
in front of the fountain at Lincoln Center,
then watched the cars drive by on Columbus
without reason to cry
and I've cried even more then.

The one year I lived on St. Marks Place
I was in grad school and cried at Cafe Orlin
with one drink for a million hours
until I'd write a poem and immediately
send it to the *New Yorker*
feeling entirely justified
because why wouldn't they want it.
It was terrible. All of it.
But I miss those days most.

The 6 train is my favorite train to cry on.

It's always late
and full of other people's fathers.
No one really looks at you

because they're so glad
they're not you,
and of course because they know
that being anyone is a tragedy
like the MTA itself.

There's something productive
about crying in New York.
It's almost like crying alone in your apartment
but you can cruise strangers
and run errands at the same time.

Once I was so exhausted
I started crying in the middle of a drink
with my friend Rachel
at the Beagle (which is closed now),
but I was telling her how people
always ask poets to do things for free
as if we don't have to pay rent
or attend to our loneliness.

Please pay poets, people.
Please pay poets more than anyone else.

I've also cried when I was happy
in a cab on the FDR
listening to Patti Smith
the day my first book got taken.
And again that night
when my parents asked
how much money I'd make
and what I would do next,
you know, after this poetry thing.

It turns out that next
there's more crying.

In so many gay bars
I'm going to list them:
Boiler Room, Eastern Bloc,
Nowhere, Metropolitan
and I could go on but this poem
isn't about gay crying,
just crying in general.

That reminds me how I used to cry
in Ray's Pizza (also on St. Marks Place)
and how one time a guy asked
if I had cocaine and if we could
"go somewhere more chill" to do it.

I was so confused I pretended
to stop crying and said, "No.
Can't you fucking see that I'm crying."

Then I went to Cooper Union across the street
and continued crying there but less convincingly.

Believe it or not,
I've never cried in a man's apartment.
A man I was sleeping with or about to.
They've all thought I was too detached
and should cry more. They've all been
emotionally bankrupt, to say the least.
Especially the lawyers.

Clearly none of them could picture me
crying in front of the Bowery Hotel
when I lost my wallet,
the same day I had three poems rejected
and went on an awful date,
the kind that makes you wonder
if you should stop talking to people

and just max out your credit card
at Opening Ceremony.

I've also cried in the Sunshine on Houston
(all of its theaters and the lobby)
and each time I remember
how someone once told me
it was a bathhouse, which is delightful
and makes me feel incredibly safe.

(The Sunshine is also closed now
by the way, like Opening Ceremony.
And that's what happens in New York
when you finally find a good spot to cry in.
It's more or less gone in a flash.)

Of course there've been times
when I wanted to cry and couldn't.
Moving. Waiting for test results.
Finding out someone I used to date
is now married (to a dancer
with a nice face and no talent;
good luck with that, babe!).

I don't think I should
count the times I've cried at home.
Who could anyway?
I've only had three apartments:
St. Marks Place, Houston and Allen,
and 75th and 1st Avenue.

I got that last one
being lucky one night on the A train,
when I ran into a guy
who was on the same call sheet
for a photo shoot we once did for *Out* magazine.

He told me he had a friend who had a friend
who wanted to pass the apartment down to a gay friend
because the rent was good and in a nice area.

I'm that gay friend, I said! That's me.

And I still live there—still gay—
the last time I cried being two hours ago.

Sometimes I cry walking down Prince Street
pretending I have allergies.
It's my favorite street in the city
and my favorite street in the world.

Especially the red brick surrounding the church
where on many weekends in summer
vendors set up their stands
and sell mostly odd things.

A woman almost sold me a crucifix there
in 2010 but I couldn't afford it
so we talked about past lives and Stevie Nicks,
and how *Tusk* is most certainly better than *Rumours*.

By the end of our talk she just gave it to me.
She was a painter and had great energy
and I'm sorry, I know this is not LA
but that word just does something for me.

It might be like counting
the wars America's been in
if I had to tell you
all the restaurants I've cried in.
Most of them are in the East Village
but I do love throwing a tantrum on the west side
where people are slightly more scandalized

because they're maybe a million dollars richer.
I have no idea. I have $574
in my bank account right now.

I've also cried in front of delivery people
and I never feel bad
because there's so many reasons to cry here
I know that they get it.

Besides, I tip 30%
(sometimes 35 if I'm feeling emotional)
and I'd like to take the time now
to remind people to tip well.
It says everything about you,
especially on a date.

Naturally, when I see someone crying in New York
it's like an invitation.
Like I should get to work and join them,
like we're about to do something
important together.

I do feel lucky I live here
since growing up I wasn't allowed to cry,
and if I have kids I'll definitely tell them
how useful it is
and how it costs only nothing.

You're free to cry all the time!
Please cry, everybody!
Please use your freedom!

Until one day you realize you're not free at all.
You never were to begin with.
You're just another person crying on 10th Street.

Again.

The other day I wanted to see you
like I haven't wanted anyone before.
But I was in New York
and you were in San Francisco.
I completely forgot we'd never met.
That you had left the country
and possibly the earth.
Which is how I would describe desire.

DECEMBER

Who would miss the year at this hour?
Like headlights circling suburbia.
And since there aren't directions
to the afterlife, we must put on
our coats and smile. We must be
children pressing our hands
to the ice, without apology
for our awe—the same kind
we keep trying to find
in churches and cheap hotels.
The kind we can't buy
in malls or airport bars.
I have said so many things I don't mean
it would take lives I've yet to imagine,
stepping onto another train,
a lost pair of kites hurrying,
many drinks, less expectations—
surely you know the feeling
of having to walk through the cold
without music or stars.

POEM FOR THE READER

Since we'll likely never be together
anywhere but here—what season
are you most alive in?
Is the morning blue or green?
How would you use freedom?
What part of your body do you trust the least?
Permanent rain or never-ending snow?
When are your most difficult hours?
Would you want to know who you were
before this? Why or why not?
And now that there's fire—
the bridge or the river?
More money or love?
Do you sometimes avoid happiness?
If asked, would you return?
To Earth or anywhere else?

WINTER SOLSTICE

Again it's the longest night of the year.
The city closer to a replica of movie sets.
Its garish streets announcing
what cannot be measured: silence,
who we were in mirrors, neon in the gray.
Three pigeons huddle under bar light.
A couple argues in a diner while a server
brings their check. It's unclear what history
has done to them, or even the last five minutes.
Besides, who knows what to do with love?
It may not make it through one cigarette.
And it's enough to kill you, how dark it is
how cold we seem even in our own misery
all while knowing we will miss this.
We will miss this when it ends.

JANUARY

Then one day you're in traffic
at the end of the frozen room.
The edges of your life undressing
and the actors who played you
rehearsing lines that couldn't
bring you to love. Imagine
the thankless highway
with its signs and detours
opening onto what may have been
yours and is not. You waited.
You waited. You became the same
well-made drink after six every time.
If there is a shape to movement
the bridge carries it. The body
runs and is nothing like wind.
Imagine then, on some morning
when even decision feels
hopeless—imagine if you
open the car door and go.

LSD

Everyone's alone on Mars tonight
and love sex death have left for Earth.
Part of me is still on a beach
where I lost something years ago.
Part of me on a beach
and life's playing from the beginning.
Nine hawks dividing the dusk.
Wild light through each tunnel in time.
The day I met you never ended for me.

POEM COMPOSED ON A OUIJA BOARD

YES

your face   & POSSIBLY

mine   NO

     MORE

          BRONZE ARCHES

   for anyone who wouldn't

TOUCH   you

      this FAR

from armor

           a RIVER

you slept in

     MYTH   LEGEND

        &

      absolute   SKY

FEBRUARY

There are people dying in emergency rooms
and people in love every night
before and after the feast of Saint Valentine.
Next the Atlantic will turn to solid ice.
The three strange angels will come
with your ego's last wishes
and there you'll be, thinking of ecstasy
over a cup of coffee and why anyone returned.
Love is not a fraud but there are many rumors.
People are dying without anyone to call.
How much would you pay to be touched
in the right way? Who would you think of
with your hands on some bed like an animal
and haven't we all been here,
walking through the world
waiting for someone to free us
or tie us to ourselves.
People are dying, yes
despite all our knowledge.
Regardless of touch, what we own,
everything we continue to steal.
Everyone and their miniature triumphs.
No, they can't convince me love isn't
our best invention. And why
I went into the ice to swallow more
than my body had room for.
Even afraid I opened my mouth
and I swallowed. I took it all down.
I was made by the cold.

PLACES I'VE CONTEMPLATED SUICIDE
OR SENT NUDES FROM

My bed
The bathrooms at the Frederick Hotel
Cabs
The 7-Eleven on 74th and 1st
The Museum of Modern Art
The Museum of Modern Art's Robert Gober opening in 2014
My writing desk
The stairwells of so many buildings
An elevator once
My favorite wine bar (which I won't actually name)
A few times at a friend's place
(a friend I used to sleep with
a friend who used to be a friend)
Central Park
The Marlton Hotel
The Plaza
The Starbucks on 75th and 1st
My bathtub
My bathroom
My very sad kitchen

in which I never cook
and look

how this is no longer
a list poem.

I wonder if anyone can actually tell what I am.

I wonder why it is they keep looking.

I wonder why they keep looking
and asking me to disappear at the same time.

ETHER

Everyone who goes to Paris must return.
Impossible hour. Lit night I mistook
for a girl. And I finally became
whatever moves through the grasses.
Not once was I cheated by sky.
Do not forget, do not forget
how water goes down the throat
even as the world kills
something else. Someone ready
to take your clothes off
in the middle of afternoon.
Without pity. Without any without.
And if you were born in Paris
you return to some star. And if all this
goes starless, it will go. And goes.
Wind. Wind. Wind. Wind.

The Mystery—begins one headline—
or why in looking for utopia on Earth
over 900 people were led to mass suicide in 1978.
Why some of us have never been in love and marry.
Why walking out on the past
may change as little as walking back in.
Some piece of land in the Alaska wilderness
no person has survived or seen.
As to tell—of the seconds, minutes,
stretches of time recorded between someone
being pronounced dead and returning.
What is referred to as Lazarus syndrome.
What many doctors and priests cannot explain.
Why people get up for morning
in the middle of night. At the height of pain
or atop the tallest mountain in this world
where it's possible to see three countries at once
and for many impossible to live in just one
without looking for more. Why do we think
there is more? After everything. After anyone
on this page, in this room…has maybe twenty,
fifty, surely no more than eighty years left
of this—and this again—and this in snow
or rain—even less than—the end.
Its unforgiving heat. Where whatever
we meant to become is minor. Is gone.
Like the story of everyone
who found fame and soon understood
being known is almost enough.

ORLANDO

An old dream
where a truck full of flowers
flips in the middle of the highway.

The first shots in a church. A boy
tied to a fence. The planes no one forgets
crashing that Tuesday.

Or the summer forty-nine people died dancing.

The summer I couldn't sleep.
The summer of wine, married men, almost nothing.

I understand now why people refuse the end of love.
They know all about it.

It has always been promised to them.

AMERICAN LIFE

And they congratulated themselves
on their outrage
in the new late capitalism.

BLUE MARBLE

Looking at it I can only think of my friend,
who after a long dinner has sent me the photo
taken in 1972 on the last mission to the moon,
and which I've seen hundreds of times
without awe, as if my life were apparent
and I knew exactly where it took place.
Before that we talk about love.
We talk about reasons
and ways it does not work out.
We have to do this. We admit it
so we can order another glass of wine
and forget we've done it at all.
My friends make great lovers.
I can tell by the way they offer me
their loneliness. By their devotion
to things they can't have
like the moon or the past.
The blue marble I look at
somewhat bored by its shape
when my favorite things are shapeless.
Like my friend's grace at the restaurant.
Her optimism. Her stillness.
She had just left a man or not yet,
hard to tell. It was Friday.
It could have been any month.
And it didn't matter if we
couldn't get over anything.
We weren't the type to try.

MARCH

Every time I feel close
to understanding the world
the white kettle on my stove sounds
and I rise, attending to it
with annoyance and the pleasure
of the unmade cup of tea.
This is what it's like to live in March
or perhaps always, an unconvincing word
in any context. Blue-gold on night's branches
what part do we take in the play?
Whose turn is it to perform competence
and knowledge in the absence of both?
Unable to feel anything against the wind
I know it is spring. Time tells me so.
Never (equally as unconvincing)
have I been someone with faith in order
and human law. Love is unpredictable.
Spring arrives regardless.

HISTORY

The turn in the day
when it's no longer morning.

Men I loved
and haven't spoken to in years.

What used to be St. Mark's Bookshop
at 12 St. Marks Place.

Nothing ends.

THE WEATHER OF OUR LIVES

Had we known we were always in it?
The house by the ocean
where you think of the desert
and not coming home.
What we can't admit:
how time together is an achievement
how time together dulls passion.
Or the origin. The one origin
when no pill was needed
to live with decision.
In the middle. The awful middle
where we attend to our work without choice
for the illusion of choices.
Holidays, birthdays, each summer that ends.
Abandoning the urge to be beautiful.
Taking up a routine, a religion, a drink
as to not abandon more.
And sometimes, the artifice of order
in a clean room. Outside which
someone presses their teeth
to your skin and shows
just how needed you are.
Before language delivers you
back to the world
but not without cruelty
and seldom for long.
You deserve it. You earned
this escape. Someone's tongue
and rough hands that remind you
you're here. You're a person again.

APRIL

Maybe the trees won't impress someone
looking for June or a new lover.
There are people ahead carrying flowers,
unaware of our many mistakes.
Let me imagine you now in your house
surrounded by worst-case scenarios
and rehearsed practicality.
What other animal plans their own funeral?
What animal makes room for death like we do?
My friend believes the Brontë sisters
didn't carry umbrellas since their characters
walked the moors without them.
I would like to agree. I would like
to walk the moors without anyone.
And open the window to ask for rain.
And I love the rain.

IMMORTALITY

That anything could last so long.
That we thought something would.
How anyone is who we'd be.
How we were something less.
Just the word for it—
what isn't real, what never was.
And in language, where we left a space.
And in dying, how we did leave that.

POEM WITHOUT GOD

I waited so long
with one drink at the same bar.
Finally, I stepped out to have a cigarette alone.

MAY

What can I tell you?
I'm a young man in Central Park.
A cherry blossom falls in my hair
like small cruelty.
I listen to a couple speak Dutch
knowing as little about them
as I do of my past.
Why go home at all?
The sun stays out for hours.
Kids race toy boats in the pond
and the dogs are on leashes,
tied to their humans and better behaved.
It was supposed to be a different life,
I kept reading about it.
I kept telling people I slept with
how soon we would know
(even as dread became daily)
exactly what to do with ourselves.

There were days I didn't go out
and days I couldn't remember.
Sometimes I sat at my desk
watching the trees outside blooming,
as if we had nothing in common.
They had the sun,
I had the sun through a window.
They were beginning,
I was unsure what I was.
Then one afternoon
after an early drink
I decided to get them—
alive and understated,
aware they were not
the most beautiful flowers
yet reassuringly strong.
I don't know how they gave
the illusion of order.
One that was impossible to find
talking to friends, lovers, old colleagues;
they did not talk back. The tulips.
They merely filled the room,
their purpose being to be loved
for what they were, entirely
by how I saw them. No struggle
or epiphany. No work.
And so I did. I loved them.
I was envious I could not be them.
Simple and so sudden. In a vase.

TO EVERYTHING

What will it be to die?
I can't imagine it

and have for years.
In the earliest memory of childhood

I don't stop touching the world
or asking what the day is.

Is it really what it looks like?
Do all people fall in love?

Or is there always someone searching,
unable to rest, finding nothing.

Nothing, nothing, nothing.

You too are something.
You too have made your way inside me.

Yes then. To everything.
Even an ending.

NOTES FOR MY FUNERAL

No one's allowed to tell
their sad story at my funeral.
No one's allowed to tell
my sad story at my funeral.
There must be cocaine.
Talk shit about all the people
I hated. I'll still hate them
(probably even more when I'm dead).
Play Lou Reed's "Perfect Day"
on repeat. Don't cry.
Don't be embarrassing.
It's not a good song
to do drugs to so after
play Fleetwood and take
a Xanax. Rent a room
overlooking Central Park
and get more drugs.
Invite strangers up.
Don't return desperate
texts from people who
hound you because
they're boring.
Just think about me.
Think of New York.
How the people who
never liked me never
liked me because they
always assumed I was
having too much fun.
And you know what?
I was. I loved being alive.

POEM WRITTEN IN A CAB

To the people
reading this poem, hello.
I want you to know
nothing bad will happen
as long as you're here.
Every line you see
was written in a cab.
I'm on the FDR
in the middle of winter
and the sky is suddenly bluer
than Sundays in June.
There's no reason for it.
No real science
to what will happen when
I get off at Chambers
and Broadway, wearing
gold and black sneakers
on my way to meet
a friend who is sad.
To my sad friends, hello.
For you I will be
a version of myself
I hardly remember.
I will be a lake
at the top of morning
some late afternoon into night.
And if you look away from
this page, to your right
there's the world.
I am only trying to describe it.
I will likely disappoint you
like a long-awaited date

or like last call at a bar.
The people on Water Street
are leaving work now.
Walking to shops
and to restaurants
or of course to the water—
Manhattan, you are
my favorite island by far.
And I wouldn't be a poet
if I didn't tell you
about the bridges,
there are over two thousand here—
Brooklyn, Verrazzano,
George Washington—
partial hyperbole, partial admission:
I live here for the bridges at night.
It's been so long
since I've taken a vacation
and some days I think,
how is that even possible,
how is this even my life?
I thought I'd be happier
and more handsome,
certainly better loved
and more stable
this late in the day.
But the secret with me
(as I'm sure with you too)
is that everyone thinks
I am fine. Doing great!
What's the point
of saying otherwise
really. It's so gauche
and betrays a self-pity

that probably means
you aren't getting laid.
The mood in Union Square
reminds me of a feeling
I once felt in 1995.
The park looks perfect
and deceptively true.
A gorgeous blond
is smoking a joint
and reading, not
waiting for anyone
and refusing to look up.
Maybe he will
but it just doesn't
seem like today
is the day to get
his attention.
He's already turning
the page and so focused,
whatever he's reading
it's all that he is.
And just so you know
we're in a different cab now,
in another month
with better weather—
goodbye to the past!
It's important
to look at something
you can't have
at least once a day.
Like the blond
a few lines up.
Perhaps you should
even touch it

or put it in your mouth.
When people kiss in public
it's a sign you're not alone.
Even if you're not the one
being kissed, there's something
obviously human about it.
And to be obvious is boring
except for real sentiment
or standing naked
in front of someone.
We're all either kissing
or pissing on each other.
Everything in between
is too safe to comment on
and not poetry in the least.
Once I was 19
and now I'm 33.
I used to prefer autumn
but spring has made me an adult.
The silence on Charles Street
is charming, even though it's
nothing like the silence I know,
which can't be compared to
a street or anything modern
despite this being
a New York poem.
Still, I'm going to try
because what else is there to do
other than work
and down gin and tonics.
There's a minute
right before the cab
drops me off
when I think—*don't stop,*

take me anywhere else.
Just keep driving!
I have it all wrong.
I have it all wrong
but I'm somehow alive.
Some things never change
and why would you want them to.
Like Katz's deli,
where I still haven't eaten
but take comfort
in knowing it's there.
Or the Flatiron building
where I've been once or twice,
and where my friend
Dorothea and I took photos
in an elevator and talked about
why it's important
to keep going no matter what.
Poets are doing this constantly
and it's one way of showing people
possibility is real and invented.
It has to come from the self!
It doesn't just show up one day.
You have to leave your house
to make eyes with someone
over a kale salad. Sometimes
you have to dye your hair blond
to remember you're truly a brunette.
Whenever I see people
crying on First Avenue
I think of the times
I've cried on First Avenue—
which is, by all standards,
a great avenue to cry on.

Like Janis Joplin's
"Get It While You Can"
is a great song and one
that's extended my life
on many occasions.
Not scientifically
but undeniably spiritually.
And stay with me now
as this is the part of the poem
where I'm trying to tell you
life is better than death
and more ridiculous too.
This is hard to know
given the day or the season,
but I have to trust myself
since I'm likely
the most neurotic poet
in the room, and maybe someone
you'll know in another life
when we come back as dogs.
The thing is, the world
will continue without us
just as this poem will continue
even if there's no one
to read what it says.
Please keep reading.
I care so much that you do.
I want to be in rooms
and cabs together,
listening to everything
that's ever happened to us
until some point in the story
when all the details
are out of the way

and there's nothing left to say
except the simplest things.
I don't know what they are
but on Bleecker Street
at half past noon on a Wednesday
two boys are pointing
at a billboard
or studying the sky.
Whatever they're thinking of,
it's not about the end of the world.
One of them is wearing
an orange hat and the other
has a button on his backpack
that says "M E O W."
Exactly! Only yesterday
I spoke to everyone like a cat.
Which is to say, I was mysterious
and pleasing to myself.
I stopped confusing
my body for a weapon
but my body has never
impressed me.
I'm Slavic, after all.
I don't believe in
self-love, which is
a kind of American sadness
that often feels
desperate and dull.
It's powerful to feel
you can change
even small things,
even things that don't
seem to matter at all.
Like the arch of your eyebrows

or the color of your lips
(both of which,
now that I think of it,
are very important and real).
Like being at a party
and for less than a second
feeling like someone entirely new.
I have never wanted to be myself.
What a ludicrous obligation!
Having a fantasy
is the least sad thing there is
and the only thing
that gets me out of bed.
Which makes me think
I should sit down
and write a list
of my fantasies
or at least the things
I love about the world.
Maybe the list will be so long
I'll call it "Love"
and turn it into a book,
allowing me to feel
justified in not taking more cabs
as a way to finish this poem.
In any case, whenever
I'm in California
I want to be in New York.
And whenever
I'm in New York
I'd rather be in London
because the rain is like light there,
it has this way of calming me down.
It's 9:14 pm

and the cab I'm in now
is on West 8th Street
almost at the Marlton Hotel
where I'm going on a date.
I have no choice but to follow
my idea of romance,
which as it turns out
means checking my hair
on my phone, like a mirror,
and after too many drinks
telling a man that my favorite word
is *bijou*—French for jewel.
Haven't I suffered enough
terrible dates! Couldn't this
be the one that changes
my life and comes with
a house in the Hamptons.
I can never fall asleep
with a stranger in bed
unless it's their own bed
and feels like the aisle seat
on a flight to Europe.
Which is to say—
there's an escape!
Or at least a way
to attend to your needs.
There's a freedom in hotel bars
when telling the bartender a secret
or switching up your drink
can remind you life isn't over.
That maybe it's just stalled for a while.
Usually my drink is champagne
or prosecco. Red wine
with my friend Will,

Diet Coke with Melissa,
and anything anywhere
with my longest friend
Rachel, who everyone knows
wears all black. Marya
does this lovely thing
where she asks for a glass of seltzer
and pours half of it in her rosé.
I really think she's invented
something necessary,
she's a Pisces after all.
And Deborah is classic.
I find her commitment
to cocktails an admirable choice.
I can never remember
which one exactly
because I'm always looking
at her hair, which has never
looked bad in the ten years
I've known her, and that's glamour.
If I had to define glamour
that's what I'd say it is.
Now there's no smooth way
to make this transition
but I'm in another cab again,
weeks later, trying to remember
who that guy from the date even was,
or why I said I'd text but never did,
as it usually happens with me.
I'm very close to taking out a loan
because of these cab rides.
If any patrons or arts organizations
are reading this, feel free
to send me a check or give me a call.

My number is 248 760 3425.
I think one thing
people misunderstand about me
is how ironic I am
in almost every aspect of life.
I can barely put on pants
to smoke a cigarette
but I'm absolutely dedicated
to writing a good sentence.
I wonder what my mother is doing
at exactly this moment.
I wonder if the L train
has ever taken anyone
where they needed to go.
When I was younger
all I wanted was to be taken seriously.
A serious poet! Why not.
Now I realize being taken seriously
is as arbitrary as how long you live.
I would gladly trade wisdom for youth.
Or beauty. Or the way I stood
in the corner at parties,
always complaining how boring
they were, how we should have gone
somewhere else or maybe
shouldn't have gone out at all.
Please go to parties, everyone.
Even if it's just to see
people you dread
drinking very warm beer.
Sometimes there's justice
in the world! And sometimes
you end up being
that dreadful person

drinking warm beer
and hating yourself.
I can't believe my fare is
already 17 dollars.
We're stuck in traffic
on 28th and 2nd
and I'm going to be late
but making it across town
with feeling, no less!
My driver just told me
he's Russian and I said
"oh great, I'm Bulgarian,
where in Russia exactly?"
He found this absurd
because he laughed
and said "Moscow,"
and now he's asking me
when it was that I came to America
and I'm telling him
in this roundabout way
how I was six and how
it was very hard on my parents
because we were poor
and I was the only one
who spoke English.
But I'll leave that
for later. Or never.
I'll leave you with a few
thoughts on the imagination
because the imagination
is a wild thought
and more honest
than biography.
What's happened to us

is unimportant.
Terrible things
happen to people
all the time.
It's about the day
and more than the day.
It's everything between me
and my cab driver from Moscow,
getting me to my meeting
without a hint of panic or luck.
"How long have you
lived here," I ask
and he says thirty years
which is crazy to me.
"Only twelve," I tell him.
But I actually love this so much
because for a second I'm young
in this cab, or at least
someone younger.
There's a loud bang
on Madison and I remember
that tomorrow's my birthday.
Oh god. Once again.
November 30, 1984.
It's been a while
and it's been a lot.
It's been romantic
but I definitely want more.
I have no plans
yet can easily make them.
There's rarely enough money
but surely it's possible
to walk down the street
and have coffee alone.

I put in my headphones
and listen to Nico's
"These Days"
before my meeting.
It's such a good song,
I can't believe that it's real.
So good in fact,
that for however long
I forget about everything.
New York is New York.
My life is decidedly mine.
Then I start worrying I haven't
worn enough sunscreen
and will someday die of
cancer. I start worrying
I won't die of cancer
but be forgotten and old.
I'm so dramatic.
I'm not even a poet.
I'm really an actor.
And almost at 34 now,
yes, I do think
I look great for my age.
I ate an egg and an orange
for breakfast. My beard
is quite long and still
very well groomed.
It's incredible really,
even to me, who rarely
feels accomplished
or takes compliments,
that anyone can make it this far.

"Living on Earth" borrows the phrase "animal soup of time" from Allen Ginsberg's "Howl."

"Love" is included here, although not in its entirety. The poem is endless. For its continuing form please visit @apoemcalledlove on Twitter, where one line is added each day.

"June" borrows the line "It's Sunday and the trains run on time" from Frank O'Hara's poem "June 2, 1958."

"July" borrows the phrase "the free space of the sky" from Walt Whitman's "A July Afternoon by the Pond."

"August" borrows the phrases "So this is love" and "Perhaps they were right in putting love into books" from William Faulkner's novel *Light in August*.

"September" borrows the phrase "no one exists alone" from W.H. Auden's poem "September 1, 1939."

"October" borrows the sentence fragment "the extremely insignificant position I have in this important world" from the journals of Virginia Woolf as written on October 23, 1917.

"November" borrows the line "It was always November there" from John Ashbery's poem "The Chateau Hardware."

"A True Account of Talking to the Moon at Fire Island" borrows its opening and closing lines from Frank O'Hara. The title is also adapted from O'Hara's poem "A True Account of Talking to the Sun at Fire Island."

"December" borrows the phrase "a lost pair of kites hurrying" from Truman Capote's short story "A Christmas Memory."

"January" borrows the line "At the end of the frozen room" from Weldon Kees's poem "January."

"February" borrows the line "Next the Atlantic will turn to solid ice" from Anne Sexton's poem "February 17th."

"March" borrows the line "What part do we take in the play" from W.B. Yeats's *A Full Moon in March*.

"April" borrows the line "And I love the rain" from Langston Hughes's poem "April Rain Song."

"May" adapts the lines "I am a young man, / In Central Park" from Amy Lowell's poem "May Evening in Central Park."

"Poem Written in a Cab" was written from September 2017 to August 2019. The constraints I gave myself were that I could only write it in the Notes app of my iPhone whenever I was in a cab.

ACKNOWLEDGMENTS

Thank you to everyone at Copper Canyon Press.

Thank you to the editors of the following publications where some of these poems first appeared, at times in earlier versions: *The American Poetry Review, BuzzFeed, The Cincinnati Review, Columbia Journal, Harvard Review, The Iowa Review, KGB Bar Online Literary Review, The New Yorker, The New York Times, The Paris Review, Poetry,* and *Town & Country.*

Thank you to the Felix Gonzalez-Torres Foundation for giving us the rights to use his work on the cover.

Thank you to New York City.

Thank you to my friends.

And thank you for reading.

If you'd like to answer the questions in "Poem for the Reader," email them to loveandotherpoems@gmail.com. I'll read them.

ABOUT THE AUTHOR

Alex Dimitrov is the author of *Together and by Ourselves*, *Begging for It*, and the online chapbook *American Boys*. With Dorothea Lasky, he is the co-author of *Astro Poets: Your Guides to the Zodiac*. He lives in New York.

Poetry is vital to language and living. Since 1972, Copper Canyon Press has published extraordinary poetry from around the world to engage the imaginations and intellects of readers, writers, booksellers, librarians, teachers, students, and donors.

WE ARE GRATEFUL FOR THE MAJOR SUPPORT PROVIDED BY:

THE PAUL G. ALLEN
FAMILY FOUNDATION

 amazon *literary partnership*

4
CULTURE

the **point**
envision · enact · evolve

Lannan

 ART WORKS.

National
Endowment
for the Arts
arts.gov

A&
OFFICE OF ARTS & CULTURE
SEATTLE

WASHINGTON STATE
ARTS COMMISSION

TO LEARN MORE ABOUT UNDERWRITING
COPPER CANYON PRESS TITLES,
PLEASE CALL 360-385-4925 EXT. 103

WE ARE GRATEFUL FOR THE MAJOR SUPPORT PROVIDED BY:

Anonymous

Jill Baker and Jeffrey Bishop

Anne and Geoffrey Barker

In honor of Ida Bauer, Betsy
  Gifford, and Beverly Sachar

Donna and Matthew Bellew

Will Blythe

John Branch

Diana Broze

John R. Cahill

The Beatrice R. and Joseph A.
  Coleman Foundation

The Currie Family Fund

Laurie and Oskar Eustis

Austin Evans

Saramel Evans

Mimi Gardner Gates

Gull Industries Inc. on behalf of
  William True

The Trust of Warren A. Gummow

Carolyn and Robert Hedin

Bruce Kahn

Phil Kovacevich and Eric Wechsler

Lakeside Industries Inc. on behalf
  of Jeanne Marie Lee

Maureen Lee and Mark Busto

Peter Lewis and Johnna Turiano

Ellie Mathews and Carl Youngmann
  as The North Press

Larry Mawby and Lois Bahle

Hank and Liesel Meijer

Jack Nicholson

Gregg Orr

Petunia Charitable Fund and
  adviser Elizabeth Hebert

Gay Phinny

Suzanne Rapp and Mark Hamilton

Adam and Lynn Rauch

Emily and Dan Raymond

Jill and Bill Ruckelshaus

Cynthia Sears

Kim and Jeff Seely

Joan F. Woods

Barbara and Charles Wright

Caleb Young as C. Young Creative

The dedicated interns and
  faithful volunteers of
  Copper Canyon Press

The Chinese character for poetry is made up of two parts:
"word" and "temple." It also serves as pressmark for
Copper Canyon Press.

The poems are set in Verdigris.
Book design and composition by Phil Kovacevich.

CPSIA information can be obtained
at www.ICGtesting.com
Printed in the USA
JSHW051349180222
23018JS00003B/11

9 781556 595998